MICROSOFT® OFFICE WORD® 2007 UPDA

GREGG
College Keyboarding
& Document Processing

OBER
JOHNSON
ZIMMERLY

MAP

Home

Lessons 1-120
10th Edition

Scot Ober
Ball State University

Jack E. Johnson
University of West Georgia

Arlene Zimmerly
Los Angeles City College

Visit the *College Keyboarding* Web site at www.mhhe.com/gdp

**McGraw-Hill
Higher Education**

Boston   Burr Ridge, IL   Dubuque, IA   New York   San Francisco   St. Louis
Bangkok   Bogotá   Caracas   Kuala Lumpur   Lisbon   London   Madrid   Mexico City
Milan   Montreal   New Delhi   Santiago   Seoul   Singapore   Sydney   Taipei   Toronto

The McGraw-Hill Companies

McGraw-Hill
Higher Education

Home (Student) Software with Installation Guide to accompany
Gregg College Keyboarding & Document Processing: Microsoft® Word 2007 Update, Lessons 1-120, Tenth Edition
Scot Ober, Jack E. Johnson, and Arlene Zimmerly

Published by McGraw-Hill, a business unit of The McGraw-Hill Companies, Inc., 1221 Avenue of the Americas, New York, NY 10020. Copyright © 2008 by The McGraw-Hill Companies, Inc.
All rights reserved.

1 2 3 4 5 6 7 8 9 0 IPP/IPP 0 9 8 7

ISBN   978-0-07-336837-5
MHID   0-07-336837-7

www.mhhe.com

Contents

Chapter 1 — Getting Started

1.1 | Welcome to GDP

Gregg College Keyboarding & Document Processing (GDP) is a Windows-based program designed for use with the *Gregg College Keyboarding & Document Processing™ 10th Edition* textbook. The software and textbook mirror and reinforce each other. From new key presentations to advanced word processing, all exercises in the textbook are included in one all-encompassing program. For document processing exercises, GDP can link to Microsoft Word® 2000, 2002, 2003 and 2007.

GDP includes the following features to help you achieve keyboarding proficiency:

- An intuitive, Web-based interface provides a contemporary learning environment for today's high-tech office and makes it easy for you to use the software even if you have limited computer experience.
- Multimedia "hand" demonstrations for new key presentations allow you to visualize correct finger placement on home row keys while still being able to see all of the keys on the keyboard.
- Interactive language arts tutorials help you build the traditional language arts skills that are essential for effective business communications.
- The MAP (Misstroke Analysis and Prescription) program diagnoses accuracy problems and provides intensive, individualized remediation.
- The tennis game and the pace car game reinforce keyboarding skills in a fun setting.
- Bilingual English/Spanish instruction screens and powerful distance-learning features meet the needs of an increasingly diverse student population.

1.2 | System Requirements

To run GDP, your system must meet the following minimum requirements:

- Pentium III CPU or higher

- Microsoft® Me®, 2000®, XP®, or Vista®
- 128 MB RAM required for Windows XP or Vista systems.
- Hard disk drive
- Network compatible; the software can be installed on a network so that multiple users may access it at the same time. It will be compatible with most networks, including Novell Netware 5 and Windows NT 2000 servers.
- CD-ROM drive (8X or faster) required for installing the program and using Home version
- Graphics adapter, SVGA or higher; 800 x 600, True Color (24-bit or 32-bit), or High Color (16-bit) modes
- SVGA color monitor
- Data will be stored on the hard disk, data diskette, or removable media such as a Zip disk for the Home version.
- Netscape Navigator 7.2 or Microsoft Internet Explorer 7.0

GDP student data can be stored in a student subdirectory on the hard disk, on a network or virtual network connection, or on floppy disk or other removable media.

| 1.3 | ## Required Materials |

To complete instructional activities in the program, you will need the following:

- *Gregg College Keyboarding & Document Processing™ 10th Edition* textbook for the appropriate lessons.
- *Microsoft® Word 2007 Manual for Gregg College Keyboarding & Document Processing 10th Edition, Lessons 1–120* (or the manual that corresponds to your version of Microsoft® Word.)
- A blank disk, if you want to store your work on floppy disks; or removable media such as a Zip disk.

1.4 | Installing GDP

GDP is designed to accommodate a host of different instructional needs and computing environments. The Home version, which is covered in this User's Guide, allows an individual student to work on GDP off campus. This is a single-user version of GDP, and it can be installed on either a standalone or an Internet and e-mail connected (distance-learning) computer.

Note | This User's Guide does not cover the Campus version of GDP. The Campus version has its own User's Guide, which is included in the GDP Campus version package.

To install the Home version of GDP on your computer:

1. Turn on the computer and start Windows.
2. Put the GDP Home version CD-ROM in the CD-ROM drive.
3. Open the Start menu (on the Windows task bar) and choose *Run*.... In the Open blank, type **d:\setup** (please note that the CD-ROM drive could be e:\ on some computers). Click **OK**. The InstallShield Wizard loads, then the Welcome dialog box displays. Click **Next** to continue.
4. In the License Agreement dialog box (Figure 1-1), click **I accept**… to accept the terms of the license agreement. Click **Next** to continue. Note: You must accept the license agreement to continue with the installation process.

Figure 1-1.
License Agreement
Dialog Box

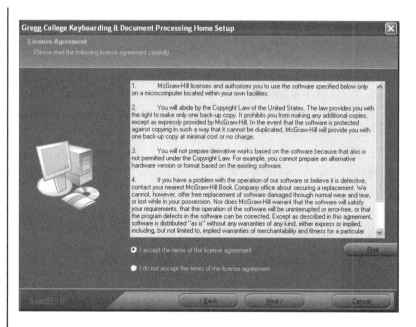

5. In the Select Destination Location dialog box (Figure 1-2), choose the local hard-disk location where you want to install the GDP software. Click **Browse** to select a location different from the default. After you select a location, click **Next**.

Figure 1-2.
Select Destination
Location Dialog Box

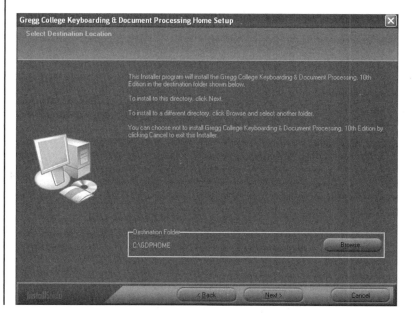

6. In the Select Student Data Location dialog box (Figure 1-3), choose an option and click **Next**.

- Select **Save student data on other media** (the default) to store student work in a data directory on the local hard disk or on other removable media such as a Zip disk. If you choose this option, the Select Student Data Path dialog box will open once you click the **Next** button.

- Select **Save student data on floppy disk A:** if the student will store work on a floppy disk in drive A.

- Select **Save student data on floppy disk B:** if the student will store work on a floppy disk in drive B.

Figure 1-3.
Select Student Data
Location Dialog Box

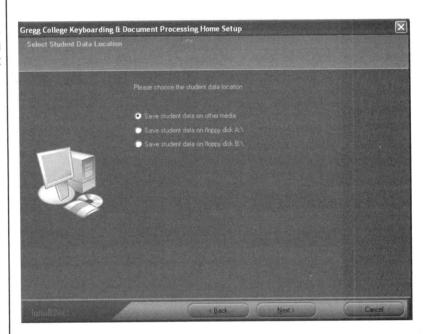

7. In the Select Student Data Path dialog box (Figure 1-4), you specify the location where student data will be stored (if you chose to save student data on other media in the previous dialog box). Click **Next** to accept the default destination folder (C:\GDPDATA), or click **Browse** to select a different location and then click **Next**.

Figure 1-4.
Select Student Data
Path Dialog Box

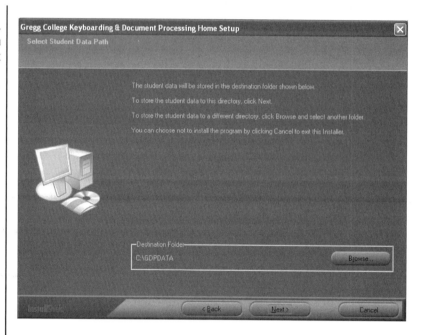

8. The installer copies the file to the workstation and displays the Install Complete dialog box. Click **Finish**.

When you complete the Home installation, a Keyboarding program group opens on the desktop with the following icon for starting GDP:

1.5 | About Student Data Files

The location of your data files is specified during the GDP10 installation procedure. Your work in GDP can be stored on floppy disks or other removable media, or on your local hard-disk drive. In any case, you will need approximately 5 MB of disk space.

1.5.1 Backing up Student Data Files

Remember to back up your data files regularly.

- If you use floppy disks to store your work, make back-up copies of your data disks on a regular basis.

- If you are storing your data on a hard-disk drive, it is important to make regular back-ups of the GDP data directory and the GDP program directory and all of its subdirectories. Failure to do so could result in data loss or corruption in the event of a power outage or other unforeseen system problems.

1.5.2 If You Are Using GDP Both on Campus and at Home

If you store your data files on a floppy disk and use GDP both on campus and at home, you should use the same floppy disk in both locations. If your data files are stored on the network on campus, you must use GDP's Import/Export feature to make sure that data files are up-to-date in both locations. For more information, see 2.6 Importing and Exporting Student Data on page 23.

1.6 About This User's Guide

The rest of this User's Guide provides the information you need to operate GDP.

- Chapter 2 provides an overview of how GDP works, including detailed instructions for starting the program and registering, specifying your settings, working on GDP exercises, accessing exercises outside of lessons, viewing and printing your work, and using GDP's distance-learning features. Chapter 2 also provides descriptions of all the types of exercises included in GDP.

- Chapter 3 is a reference guide, listing brief descriptions of all menu options, toolbar buttons, and shortcut keys. The reference guide also describes scoring and error marking.

- Chapter 4 is a troubleshooting guide, which lists common problems and suggested solutions.

- The Index provides a quick way to look up specific information in this User's Guide.

Program Overview

Gregg College Keyboarding & Document Processing (GDP) is a Windows-based program with distance-learning features that is designed for use with the *Gregg College Keyboarding & Document Processing Lessons 1-120, 10th Edition* textbook. The software and textbook mirror and reinforce each other. From new key presentations to advanced document processing, all exercises in the textbook are included in one all-encompassing program. For document processing exercises, GDP links to Microsoft Word®. Distance-learning features such as Upload and e-mail facilitate student data transfer and communication between students and instructors. Student work is recorded, is scored, and can be reviewed in the Student Portfolio.

Program Structure

Lessons

Every lesson (with the exception of Lesson 1) begins with a Warmup that should be keyed as soon as students are settled at the keyboard. All alphabet, number, and symbol keys are introduced in the first 20 lessons. Drill lines in this section provide the practice necessary to achieve keyboarding skills.

Skillbuilding sections are found in every lesson, and can be accessed directly from the GDP button toolbar. Each drill presents a variety of different activities designed to improve speed and accuracy. Skillbuilding exercises include Technique Timings, Diagnostic Practice, Paced Practice, Progressive Practice, MAP (Misstroke Analysis and Prescription), Sustained Practice, and Timed Writings.

Many lessons also include a Pretest, Practice, and Posttest routine that identifies speed and accuracy needs and measures improvement.

All of the activities contained within the lessons are also available from the navigation menu. Click the **Skillbuilding**, **Language Arts**, **Timed Writings**, **MAP**, or **Games** buttons to open the menus and directly access these activities.

Student Portfolio

All of your scores and text are stored in a portfolio that you can access at any time other than when you are working on an exercise. Your Student Portfolio is a summary report listing all the exercises and exercise scores for activities you have attempted. Detailed Reports display the scored text for exercises selected from the Student Portfolio.

Distance-Learning

You can communicate with your instructor and classmates by clicking the **E-mail** button and using GDP's e-mail feature. Use the Upload feature to send your GDP data files to the Instructor Management Web site and to receive information from your instructor (for example, grades and instructor comments). Note: To receive grades and comments from your instructor in a distance-learning environment, you must download your grades using the Student Web Site. Please go to Section 2.7.4 of this document to review the Student Web Site.

Web Access

Your school Web site, or any other Web site your instructor chooses can be directly accessed by clicking the **Web** button on the GDP navigation toolbar. Note: In the Home version of GDP, you must specify the Web link URL in your Settings (found in the Options drop-down menu).

Reference Manual

Click **Reference Manual** on the toolbar or from the *Help* menu to access a separate Help system that provides formatting instructions and examples of the types of documents taught in GDP.

2.1 | Logging On for the First Time

Here is the procedure when accessing GDP for the first time:

1. Turn on the computer and start Windows.
2. If using a floppy disk to store your data, put a floppy disk in the floppy drive.
3. From the Start menu (on the Windows task bar), choose *Programs* and point to *Keyboarding*.
4. Select

5. The title screen displays for several seconds, followed by the registration screen (Figure 2-1). (To advance to the registration screen immediately, you can click anywhere on the title screen.) When accessing the GDP Home version for the first time, you will be asked to register your first and last name ("e-mail address" and "class" are optional) in the appropriate fields and then click **Save**. Subsequently when accessing the GDP Home version, you will be taken directly to the Lessons menu (there is no log on screen in the GDP Home version).

If you selected removable media or a floppy disk drive for data storage in the Home version of GDP (during installation) and you don't have it inserted when accessing GDP, you will be prompted with the following: "Please insert your student data disk and click **OK**. If you have not yet created your student data diskette, then click the **New Student** button." (If this is your first time accessing GDP, you will want to insert your diskette and click on the **New Student** button.)

Figure 2-1.
Registration Screen

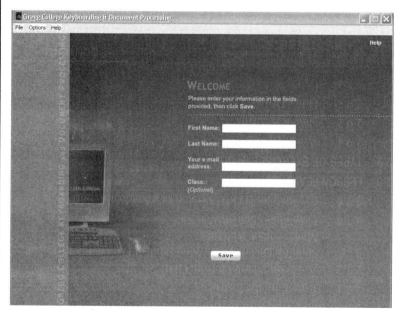

6. Complete the registration information on the log on screen and click **Save**. Note: If you are a distance-learning student, your e-mail address must be identical to the one your instructor used to register you on the Instructor Management Web site for the Upload feature to work properly. If you enter it incorrectly, you can change it later. See 2.2 Specifying Your Settings. Your first and last name will be sent to the Instructor Management Web site, so be sure they are typed correctly. See 2.7.3 Sending Distance-Learning Student Data to the Instructor Management Web site.

7. GDP registers your information, and the Tutorial pops up in a window on the screen. The Tutorial provides first-time users an overview of how GDP works.

8. Before you start working you need to specify your settings so that GDP works properly with your system. See 2.2 Specifying Your Settings, below.

9. Now you are ready to begin working in GDP. To do so, select a lesson from the Lessons menu, which displays next. For information about working on GDP exercises, see 2.3 Working on Lesson Exercises on page 14.

| *Note* | Subsequently when you start GDP, the program will take you directly to the Lessons menu and open the lesson upon which you last worked. If you installed GDP for use with a floppy disk and do not put the disk into the floppy disk drive before starting GDP, you will be prompted to insert the diskette. The prompt will ask you to insert your student data diskette and click **OK** or, if you haven't created your student data diskette yet, to click the **New Student** button. Insert your data diskette and click **OK**. |

2.2 | Specifying Your Settings

Your settings control how GDP works on your system. To specify your settings:

1. Select *Settings...* on the Options drop-down menu to open the Settings dialog box (Figure 2-2).

Figure 2-2.
Settings Dialog Box

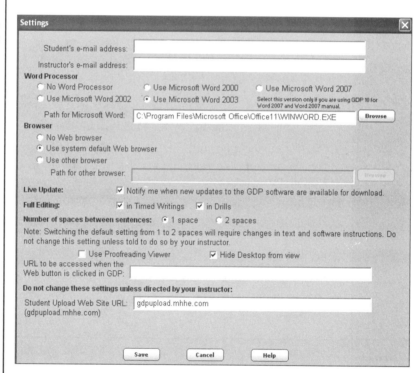

2. Review the settings and make any necessary changes.

Student's e-mail address	This is the address you entered when you initially registered within GDP. If your address changes after initial registration, you can make the change in the Settings dialog box.
Instructor's e-mail address	This is your instructor's address, which your instructor should be able to provide to you.
Word Processor	If your computer does not have Microsoft Word 2000, 2002, 2003, or 2007, then **No Word Processor** should be selected. In this case, you will not be able to do the word processing exercises in GDP. Select the correct version of Microsoft Word and specify its full path.
Browser	If **Use system default Web browser** is selected (the default), GDP will launch the system's default Web browser when you access the campus Web site. If **No Web browser** is selected, you will not be able to access the campus Web site from GDP. If you want to access the campus Web site through GDP using a browser other than your system's default browser, **Use other browser** should be selected and the full path to it

	specified. If you do not know the full path, click **Browse** to find it.
Live Update	If this box is checked (the default), you will be notified when new GDP software updates are available for download. After you access GDP, if there is a new update available for download, the Live Update dialog box will display. If this feature is deselected, you will not receive Live Update messages.
Full Editing: inTimed Writings	If this box is checked (the default), you will be able to edit text in timed writings. If unchecked, editing will be disabled during timed writings.
Full Editing: in Drills	If this box is checked (the default), you will be able to edit text in drills. If unchecked, editing will be disabled during drills.
Number of spaces between sentences	Click on the appropriate radio button to identify whether you will use one space or two spaces following punctuation at the end of a sentence (the default is **1 Space**). **Note**: Switching the default setting from 1 to 2 spaces will require changes in text and software instructions. Do not change this setting unless told to do so by your instructor.
Use Proofreading Viewer	If this box is checked (this is **not** the default; you must select it to turn it 'on'), you will be able to view your scored text while editing a document so you can see where your errors occurred.
Hide Desktop from View	If this box is checked (the default), the **Hide Desktop from View** feature will block out the desktop behind the GDP window, while still providing access to the Start menu and task bar (in the Home version, you access the Start menu and task bar only by minimizing GDP). You must deselect this feature in order to turn it 'off'.
URL to be accessed when the Web button is clicked in GDP	If your instructor would like you to be able to access the campus Web site from GDP, he or she will provide you the correct URL to enter here.
Student Upload Web Site URL	You should not change this setting unless specifically instructed to do so by McGraw-Hill. This is the URL used to upload your data when using the Distance-Learning option.

3. When finished working with settings, click **Save** to record changes and close the Settings dialog box.

2.3 | Working on Lesson Exercises

Once you access GDP, the Lessons menu (Figure 2-3) displays the list of exercises in the current lesson. If you are using GDP for the first time, Lesson 1 exercises are listed. If you have worked with GDP previously, the exercise list is for the lesson on which you last worked. A ■ precedes exercises that have been completed. A ◣ precedes exercises that have been started but not completed.

Figure 2-3.
Lessons Menu

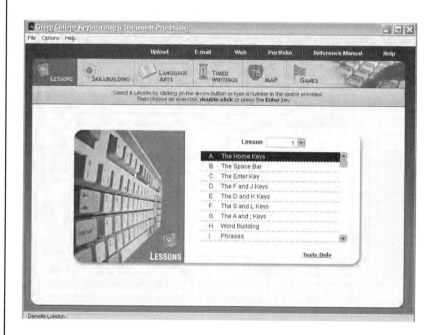

To work on an exercise:

1. Select the lesson you want to open.
   - Type the lesson number into the Lesson text box.

   or

   - Open the Lesson Text Box by clicking the ▼ button; then scroll up or down the lesson numbers.

2. Select the exercise you want to work on.
   - Highlight the name of the exercise and press **Enter** on your keyboard.

   or

- Double-click the name of the exercise.

3. Read the introductory or instruction screen(s) and turn to the appropriate page in the textbook. Type the text as instructed, and click the **Next** button at the bottom of the screen to go to the next screen in the exercise. (For more information about the exercise screen layout, see 2.3.1 Exercise Screen Layout.)

4. When you click the **Next** button at the end of an exercise, GDP goes to the next exercise in the lesson. At the end of the last exercise for a particular lesson, GDP returns to the Lessons menu.

Pressing the **Esc** key allows you to exit an exercise at any time. You can exit the program at any point by selecting *Exit GDP* on the File menu or clicking the close button (☒) at the top right.

Note | If you are a distance-learning student, you can send your data to the Instructor Management Web site at any time by clicking the **Upload** button on the toolbar. Your instructor must have registered you on the Instructor Management Web site before you can upload your data. When you log off GDP as a distance-learning student, GDP automatically prompts you to update your data on the Instructor Management Web site if you have done any work in GDP since your last update. For more information on uploading data to the Instructor Management Web site, see 2.7.3 Sending Distance-Learning Student Data to the Instructor Management Web Site on page 26.

2.3.1 Exercise Screen Layout

Exercise screens have the same basic layout throughout the program (see Figure 2-4).

Figure 2-4.
Exercise Screen
Layout

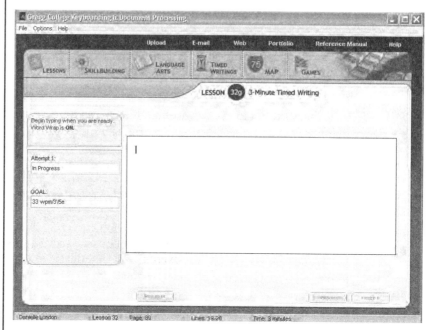

● **Title bar:** The title bar includes the program name and the standard window control menu (to the left) and the minimize, maximize and close buttons (to the right).

❷ **Menu bar:** The menu bar lists all of the drop-down menus. (For more information, see "Drop-Down Menus," later in this chapter.

❸ **Toolbar:** The toolbar includes buttons for frequently used features and on-screen guidance. (For more information, see 3.2 GDP Toolbar on page 47.)

❹ **Exercise header:** The exercise header specifies information about the current exercise, such as the speed and accuracy goals for a timed writing and scores on various attempts at the exercise. Goals and scores are noted as follows: number of words/number of minutes/number of errors (for example, "33wpm/3'/5e" indicates 33 words per minute for 3 minutes, with 5 errors).

❺ **Navigation menu:** The navigation menu running across the screen directly under the Toolbar includes icons for accessing GDP's activities by lesson and by activity type.

❻ **Body of the screen:** The body of the screen provides instructions or an area for typing text.

❼ **Status bar:** The status bar specifies your name, lesson number, and textbook page. Line numbers and length of a timed writing are indicated when applicable.

❽ Previous and Next buttons: These buttons in the bottom right corner of the screen are used to move sequentially through the screens in an exercise.

2.4 | Accessing Exercises Outside of Lessons

Typically, you will follow the textbook and use the Lessons menu to work on lesson exercises sequentially. Occasionally, your instructor may want you to access exercises by type (rather than by lesson), work on special exercises to sharpen keyboarding skills, play one of the keyboarding games, or focus on particular language arts skills for a session. In such cases, use the navigation menu running across the GDP screen directly under the Toolbar.

Use this icon to go to the Lessons menu. The Lessons menu displays all of the lessons and exercises in the textbook.

Use this icon to go to the Skillbuilding menu, which groups exercises by type and includes all of the lesson exercises except for tests, language arts exercises, and document processing exercises. The Skillbuilding menu also includes Open Timed Writings, Custom Timed Writings, Supplementary Timed Writings, Numeric Keypad Practice, MAP, the Pace Car Game, and the Tennis Game, which are not accessible from the Lessons menu.

Use this icon to go to the Language Arts menu, which displays all of the language arts exercises in the program. The Language Arts menu provides access to language arts exercises by skill area (rather than by lesson) and includes numerous interactive language arts tutorials not found in the textbook.

Use this icon to go to the Timed Writings menu, which includes all of the timed writings included in lesson exercises as well as Open Timed Writings, Custom Timed Writings, and Supplementary Timed Writings.

Use this icon to go to the MAP (Misstroke Analysis and Prescription) program, which identifies keystroking problems and prescribes remedial exercises to fix those problems.

Use this icon to go to the Games menu for quick access to the Tennis Game or Pace Car Game.

Note | The exercises accessible on the Skillbuilding, Timed Writings, and Language Arts menus work exactly the same as the corresponding exercises in the Lessons menu. The navigation menu simply provides a different way to access the exercises.

2.4.1 Linking to Word Outside of an Exercise

For documents that are included in the textbook exercises, GDP automatically links to Word 2000, 2002, 2003, or 2007, depending on the setting you selected in the Settings dialog. The *Go To Word Processor* option on the File drop-down menu is for working on other documents not included in the textbook or for printing a formatted GDP document without having to access the document through the Lessons menu. To link to the word processor outside of a textbook exercise:

1. Select *Go To Word Processor* on the File menu.
2. Word opens a new document window. You can type a new document in the blank window or open an existing document by selecting *Open* on the File menu.
3. When finished working on the document, select *Return to GDP* on the GDP menu on Word's menu bar.

Alert | The GDP program adds the GDP menu to Word's menu bar to provide you an easy, seamless route back to GDP and ensure that documents created outside of GDP exercises are saved to your data storage location. Make sure that you use this method to exit Word.

2.5 | Viewing and Printing Student Work

GDP provides a chart and two types of reports to help you keep track of your progress and review completed exercises. The chart and reports can be viewed on screen and printed.

2.5.1 Student Portfolio

Your Portfolio contains two types of reports. The Portfolio itself provides a snapshot of all exercises on which you have worked, with results and completion status for each. Detailed Reports include the scored text for any exercise on which you have worked— unless you have used the *Delete Files* option from the File drop-down menu to delete some exercises.

To access your Student Portfolio:

1. Click the **Portfolio** button on the toolbar or select the *Portfolio...* option from the File drop-down menu. Your Student Portfolio lists all of the exercises attempted. To refine this list, click the **Filter Portfolio** button to specify which exercises should appear in your Student Portfolio. The Portfolio Filter dialog box (Figure 2-5) then displays.

Figure 2-5.
Portfolio Filter
Dialog Box

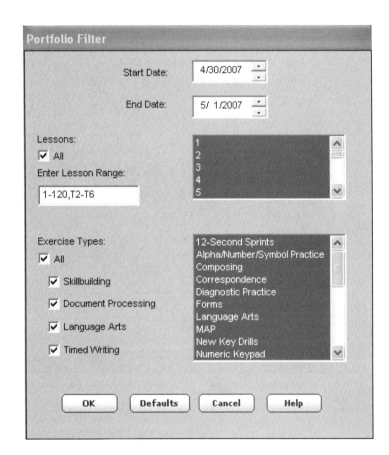

2. Specify a date range, lesson(s), and exercise type(s) to include, and then click **OK** to close the Portfolio Filter and see the filtered Student Portfolio. Click **Defaults** to select the GDP default filter (all lessons; all exercise types).

3. The Student Portfolio window (Figure 2-6) lists all of the completed exercises specified from the Portfolio Filter, one exercise per line. Each line in the Student Portfolio includes the completion date, lesson number and exercise name, score (if a scored exercise), the Total Time you spent working on the exercise, your raw grade for the exercise based on text and formatting, and your weighted average grade based on exercise type weight factors specified by your instructor. The Total Time includes time reading instruction screens, time to launch and time word processing. A question mark **(?)** indicates that a grade is not yet available. If **NA** appears in the Grade or Weighted Average columns, then your instructor has not designated that exercise as a graded activity.

An asterisk **(*)** in the first column indicates that Detailed Report text is available for the exercise. You cannot print or view text for exercises that have no text available. An **A** next to the asterisk indicates that your instructor has annotated your work.

Figure 2-6.
Student Portfolio
Window

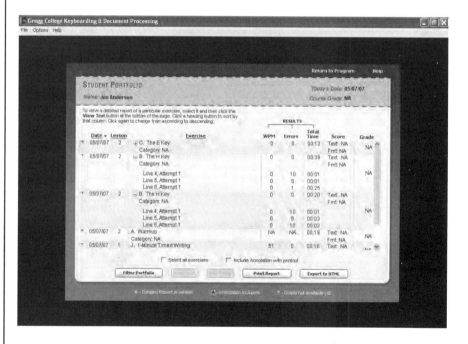

4. There are several options for viewing and printing from the Student Profile:
- To sort the report by date, lesson number, or exercise name, click on the appropriate column header. The current sort is highlighted, with an arrow indicating ascending order (up arrow) or descending order (down arrow).

- To print a copy of the Student Profile, click **Print Report**.
- To print a copy of the scored text for any exercise, click once on the lines for the desired exercise(s) (they must be preceded by an asterisk in the Date column) and then click **Print Text**.

If your instructor has requested an HTML version of your Student Profile, click **Export to HTML**. When you click the **Export to HTML** button, a *Save as* dialog will display. The dialog will include a default file name (GDPStudentProfile) and the file extension will automatically be set to "HTML files (*.htm, *.html)". Select a location where you want to save the file and click the **Save** button.

Note: It is recommended that a new, unique file name is given to each Export file. To change the file name in the *Save as* dialog box, highlight the default name in the File name field and overwrite it by typing the new file name.

Note	To select an exercise for viewing or printing, that exercise must be preceded by an * in the Date column in the Student Portfolio.

5. To view the text for any exercise (that is, get a Detailed Report), click on the desired exercise line on the Student Portfolio (they must be preceded by an asterisk in the Date column) and click **View Text**. The Detailed Report window (Figure 2-7) displays your text and scores.

Figure 2-7.
Detailed Report
Window

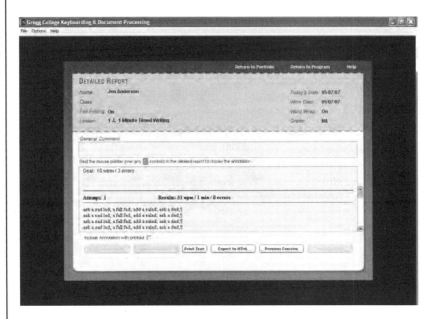

- To print the Detailed Report, click **Print Text**.
- If you selected more than one exercise for which to view text, **Next Exercise** and **Previous Exercise** buttons can be used to move among the Detailed Reports.
- Documents appear as unformatted, scored text. To view the formatted document as it appears in Word, click **View in MS Word**. You will be able to make changes to the document, but those changes will not be saved. To return to GDP, select *Return to GDP* on the GDP menu in Word's menu bar.
- To print a formatted version of the document (without viewing it in Word), click **Print in MS Word**.
- When finished viewing the Detailed Report(s), click **Return to Portfolio** to return to the Student Portfolio.

6. To exit the Student Portfolio, click **Return to Program**.

Note: The Detailed Report for any Document Processing exercise displays your Time in MS Word as well as the version of Microsoft Word in use.

2.5.2 Performance Chart

The Performance Chart graphs your progress as you type timed writings. To view this chart, select *Performance Chart* from the File drop-down menu.

The Performance Chart window (Figure 2-8) tracks your best score for each timed writing you completed. The results are graphed in groups of 20 lessons.

The boldface numbers on either side of the chart represent speed, in words per minute. The lesson numbers are listed horizontally under the graph. The timing length appears under the lesson number. The timing length appears only for graphed timed writings.

Two bars are graphed for each timed writing: the blue bar graphs your speed score and the red bar graphs the number of errors. If you made no errors on a timed writing, there is no red bar for that timed writing. Black horizontal lines indicate the speed goal and error limit for the timed writing. A red star appears above each timed writing for which you met the speed goal within the error limit.

Figure 2-8.
Performance Chart

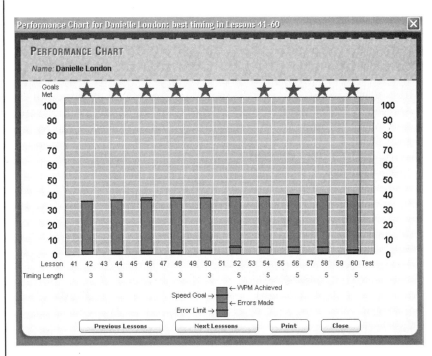

- To print a copy of the Performance Chart for the current part, click **Print**.
- To view the Performance Chart for the previous part, click **Previous Lessons**. To view the Performance Chart for the next part, click **Next Lessons**.
- To close the Performance Chart, click **Close**.

2.6 | Importing and Exporting Student Data

GDP's Import/Export feature provides an easy way for you to keep your data files current if you use GDP both on a campus LAN and at home. If you are storing your work on a fixed disk such as a local hard drive—rather than on floppy disks—your instructor can also use this feature to update your data for the gradebook.

2.6.1 Using Import/Export to Transfer Data Files Between Campus and Home

If you use GDP both on campus and at home, your data files must match in both locations. If your data is stored on a floppy disk, you can use the same floppy disk in both locations. If your data is stored on a hard disk, you should use GDP's Import/Export feature to make sure that data files are up-to-date in both locations.

To export work:

1. Select *Export Student Data...* on the File menu. The Export dialog box reminds you that this function is used to move work from one computer to another. To update your work and upload it to the Instructor Management Web site for your instructor's review, click the **Upload** button on the toolbar. Click **OK** to continue.

2. Choose the lessons and documents to export:

   • *All Lessons* - Click *Export all lessons* if all of your work is to be exported.

   • *By Date* - To export work completed within a specific date range, click *Export lessons completed between the following dates*. To select a date range, click the month, day, or year to select it. Type the new date or use the up and down arrows at the right of the date field to change the date.

   • *By Lesson* - To export work completed for specific lessons, click *Export lessons*. To enter a lesson range, type the lesson numbers followed by commas or, for a contiguous range, type the start and end lesson numbers separated by a hyphen. The selected lessons will be highlighted in the lesson number list below. To select lesson numbers from the list, press the **Ctrl** key and click the desired lesson numbers. To select a contiguous range of lessons, press the **Shift** key and click the start and end lessons in the desired range.

   Note: Please be sure to leave the "Include Microsoft Word document files for the selected lessons" checkbox selected if you also want the Word documents to be exported. This will ensure that the document files are available in the Student Portfolio when you import the data into your alternate location.

3. To specify a location where the export file is to be stored, use the default location provided or type the path to indicate a different location or name. To browse for a folder location, click the **Browse** button, select a location from the file directory, and click **OK**.

4. If you are exporting to a floppy disk, put a floppy disk in the floppy disk drive.

5. Click **Export**. Click **Cancel** to close the Export dialog box and return to GDP.

Once the work is exported, it will need to be imported to the desired GDP workstation, for example, to the instructor's workstation or to a home computer.

To import work:

1. Select *Import Student Data...* from the File drop-down menu.

2. In the Open dialog box, select the export file (which has an ".EXP" file name extension) and click **Open**.

3. The exported data is copied to the student data storage location, overwriting existing data if the export includes the same lessons that are in the student's data files.

Note	This use of the Import/Export feature is intended for use in the Home version of GDP when you are storing your data on your home computer's hard disk. If you are using the Home version of GDP and are storing your work on floppy disks, you can simply deliver your data disks to your instructor. If you are using the Distance-Learning option available within GDP, use GDP's Upload feature (see 2.7.3 Sending Distance-Learning Student Data to the Instructor Management Web Site on page 26).

2.7 | Using GDP's Web and Distance-Learning Features

2.7.1 E-mailing the Instructor

You can send your instructor e-mail messages from within GDP if the following conditions are met:

- Your e-mail system must be MAPI compliant (for example, Microsoft Outlook and Outlook Express are MAPI-compliant; AOL and CompuServe are not),

- Your e-mail address must be correct in GDP (your e-mail address is in the Personal Information form, which is accessible from the Options drop-down menu), **AND**

- Your instructor's e-mail address must be specified correctly in your settings (see 2.2 Specifying Your Settings on page 11).

To send an e-mail message from within GDP:

1. Click the **E-mail** button on the GDP toolbar.

2. An addressed e-mail message window appears for you to type a message. Type a subject and a message.

3. When ready to send your message, click the **Send** button.

2.7.2 Accessing the Web from GDP

You can access the World Wide Web (Web) if the following settings are specified and valid: the **URL to be accessed when the Web button is clicked in GDP** and the browser. (For more information, see 2.2 Specifying Your Settings on page 11.)

To access the Web from within GDP:

1. Click the **Web** button on the GDP toolbar.

2. GDP launches your browser, establishes an online connection, and opens the Web site specified in your settings.

3. When finished browsing the Web site, you can either close the browser window or switch back to GDP using the Windows task bar.

2.7.3 Sending Distance-Learning Student Data to the Instructor Management Web Site

The Distance-Learning feature within GDP allows you to upload your GDP data files to the Instructor Management Web site and receive back information from your GDP instructors (for example, class announcements and instructor comments on specific GDP exercises). In order for the distance-learning option to work properly, the following conditions must be met:

- Your system must have a default e-mail address. The default e-mail address is the one marked with "(default)" in the Mail settings in Window's Control Panel.

  (GDP uses the system default e-mail address when uploading student data to the Instructor Management Web site.)

- Your instructor's e-mail address must be correct. Your e-mail address in your installation and the e-mail address used by your instructor to register you on the Instructor Management Web site must be identical and correct in your settings. See 2.2 Specifying Your Settings on page 11.

- Your instructor must have registered you on the Instructor Management Web site before you can upload your data.

- The e-mail address your instructor used to register you on the Instructor Management Web site matches the e-mail address in your Personal Information form. (Your e-mail address is in the Personal Information form, which is accessible from the Options menu.)

- You must complete at least one exercise.

At any time while logged on to GDP when using the Distance-Learning option, you can send updated information to the Instructor Management Web site, as follows:

1. Click the **Upload** button on the toolbar to open the Upload dialog box.

2. Choose which files to send to the Instructor Management Web site:

   - To update a complete set of data files, select *Upload all work.*

   - To send only those files that have changed since the last update, select *Upload work completed since your last update.* (This usually takes less time than uploading your full set of data files.)

3. Click **Upload Work to Student Upload Web Site**. In the Upload Work dialog box, a location is specified to store the upload file. Once the upload file is stored, click **Store the Upload File**. GDP will try to use a browser to access the Student Upload Web site, located at gdpupload.mhhe.com. This site must be accessed to finish the upload process.

When files are uploaded, GDP establishes an online connection and sends data files to the Instructor Management Web site. This process can take several minutes, depending on the amount of information that needs to be transmitted and the speed of the Internet connection.

2.7.4 Using the Student Web Site

Overview

If you are a student in a distance-learning class, you can log into the GDP Student Web Site to:

- View the class page created by your instructor
- View your portfolio and annotations from your instructor
- Download your grades and annotations from your instructor so you can import the data into your GDP software

How You are Notified About the Student Web Site

When your instructor adds your e-mail address to a class at the Instructor Management Web Site (IMWS), the IMWS generates an e-mail from your instructor to you. The e-mail tells you the name of the class to which you are registered and invites you to view the Student Web Site (SWS). The e-mail includes a link to the SWS, a password, and directions for logging on to the SWS and changing the password.

Logging On to the Student Web Site

The Student Web Site log on page displays when you link to it from your instructor's e-mail or enter the URL for the Web site directly in a browser.

The URL for the Student Web Site is: http://gdpstudent.mhhe.com.

Logging On to the Student Web Site for the First Time

If this is your first time logging on to the SWS or you have not yet uploaded student data from GDP:

1. Enter your e-mail address and the password included in the e-mail you received from the IMWS, and click **Log On**.
2. If you are enrolled in more than one GDP Version 10 class, the Web site will prompt you to select your class from the list.
3. If your instructor has already created a class page, the class page displays

upon successful log on. If your instructor has not yet created a class page, the Portfolio Filter displays.

Subsequent Log Ons to the Student Web Site

Once you complete exercises in the GDP Version 10 software and upload your work to the IMWS, your data will also be available on the SWS.

Changing a Password at the Student Web Site

To change a password, you should follow these steps:

1. Launch the Student Web Site located at http://gdpstudent.mhhe.com.
2. Enter your e-mail address and click **Change Password**.
3. Enter the password in the e-mail from the IMWS (or current password if you have previously changed it).
4. Enter your GDP password in the "Your new password" and "Retype new password" fields.
5. Click **Save** to save the changes and return to the Log On screen. You can now log on with the new password.

Requesting a Forgotten Password

If you forget your password, you can request it by following these steps:

1. Launch the Student Web Site located at http://gdpstudent.mhhe.com.

2. Click the **Forgot Password?** link on the Log On page.

3. Enter your e-mail address in the space provided and click **Submit**.

4. The SWS will send an e-mail to you with your password.

Accessing the Class Page

If your instructor has created a class page for your class, the class page will display after you log on to the Student Web Site. (**Note:** If you are enrolled in more than one GDP Version 10 class, you will first have to select a class before the class page is displayed.)

The class page can include tabs for the following information:
- Course Calendar
- Syllabus
- Handouts
- Contact Information
- Links

The information displayed on the class page depends on the sections of the class page that your instructor enables when s/he creates the class page.

You can also access the other areas of the Student Web Site from the tool bar at the top of the screen, including:

- Student Portfolio
- Download Grades
- Student Upload
- Help

Displaying the Student Portfolio on the Student Web Site

You can access your student portfolio on the Student Web Site, complete with grades and annotations your instructor has added. To display your portfolio, you should follow these steps:

1. Launch the Student Web Site located at http://gdpstudent.mhhe.com and log on (see 'Logging On to the Student Web Site' in this section for more information).

2. Click **Student Portfolio** on the tool bar at the top of the screen. The Portfolio Filter displays.

3. Modify the filter options, as needed, and click **View Portfolio**. (**Note:** Select fewer exercises to speed the display of the portfolio.)

4. The Student Portfolio displays.

Displaying a Detailed Report

To display a detailed report:

1. Display your portfolio (See 'Displaying the Student Portfolio on the Student Web Site' above).

2. Select the radio button beside an exercise and click **View Detailed Report**.

3. The Detailed Report for that exercise displays.

   a. If the detailed report is for a document processing exercise, the **View in MS Word** button is active. Click this button to display the exercise in Microsoft Word.

   b. Click **Printer-Friendly Version** to display a printer-friendly version of the report.

   c. Use the **Next Exercise** and **Previous Exercise** buttons to navigate between detailed reports without returning to the Portfolio.

d. General comments from your instructor display in the General Comments field. Annotations are represented by notepad icons in the detailed report text. Rest the mouse pointer over any notepad symbols in the detailed report to display the annotation.

Downloading Grades and Annotations from the Student Web Site

If you are a student in a distance-learning class, you can download your grades and annotations from your instructor from the Student Web Site. When you download your grades, the SWS creates an export of your work, which you can then import into your GDP software. To download your grades, you should follow these steps:

1. Launch the Student Web Site located at http://gdpstudent.mhhe.com and log on.

2. Click **Download Grades** on the toolbar at the top of the screen.

3. Instructions display indicating how to download grades and import them into the GDP software. Click the **Printer-Friendly Version** link at the bottom of the screen to print a copy of the instructions.

4. To download grades:

   a. Click the **Download Grades** button on this screen.

   b. The File Download dialog box that displays is the standard dialog box that displays when you download a file or application from the Internet. Click **Save**.

   c. A Save As... dialog box displays. Select the folder in which you want to save the Export file of your grades, make note of this location, and click **Save**. Do not change the filename.

   d. Once you have downloaded your grades, you will need to import it into your software. In order to import the file, you will need to know the location of the file. For this reason, we recommend that you save the file to your Desktop.

   e. The file will begin to download. The download dialog automatically closes when the download is complete.

5. To import your grades into your GDP software:

   a. Launch GDP as you normally would. Because you are using the Home Version, you do not have to log in.

   b. Select Import Student Data... from the File menu in your GDP software.

   c. Browse to the folder in which you saved the Export file, select the file, and click **Open**. Note: You may need to change the view of the **Open** dialog box to Details so that you can see the file extensions.

  d. Once you import your grades, you will be able to view your grades and your instructor's annotations in your GDP software.

2.7.5 Creating an HTML Version of a Student Report

Whether or not your instructor uses GDP Instructor Management (the program or the Web site), your instructor may want to view your work using a Web browser. To create an HTML version of any report in your Portfolio:

1. Open your Portfolio by clicking the **Portfolio** button, specifying report settings in the Portfolio Filter dialog box, and clicking **OK**.

2. Open the report (Student Portfolio or Detailed Report) that your instructor has requested.

3. Click the **Export to HTML** button.

4. Specify a unique file name (preferably with your name embedded) and location in the Save As dialog box.

5. Click **Save**.

Once you create the HTML file, you will need to deliver it to your instructor. If you have e-mail access (within or outside of GDP), you can send your instructor an e-mail with the HTML file attached. Otherwise, you can save the HTML file on a floppy disk and hand deliver to your instructor.

2.8 Lesson Features

Bilingual Instruction Screens

All instruction screens in GDP are available in English or Spanish (Español). By default, English is used. To switch to Spanish-language instruction screens, click the **Español** button at the bottom of the screen (in Spanish mode, the button changes to **English**; click this button to return to English instructions). Note that menus, help, and toolbars appear in English only. If there is no **Español** button at the bottom of the instruction screen, then your instructor has opted to make the Spanish text unavailable for your class. Please speak with your instructor if you need to view the Spanish text.

Technique Tips

Technique tips appear randomly in GDP to give you quick pointers on keyboarding. Technique tips appear as an animated text banner at the top of the screen.

Speed/Accuracy Goals

All timed writings include speed and accuracy goals. When you work on Pretest/Practice/Posttest exercises, your Pretest results will be used to determine whether you will use a speed or accuracy routine for the Practice component of the exercise.

Word Wrap

Some exercises are keyed in Word Wrap On mode, which means that you press the **Enter** key at the end of paragraphs only. Other exercises are to be done in Word Wrap Off mode, which means that you press the **Enter** key at the end of every line. An icon will appear on the toolbar to let you know whether Word Wrap is on or off.

Student Portfolio

All of your work in GDP is stored on a floppy disk or in a data directory on a local drive or a network server. You can view your work —scores and text—by accessing your portfolio from the File drop-down menu or from the toolbar.

Printing

The reports in your portfolio can be printed. You can print your scores in your Student Portfolio as well as your scored text for any exercise.

Scoring

Much of the work you complete in this program will be scored. The program will report your words per minute (wpm) speed and the number of errors you make, as well as achievement of speed and accuracy goals.

One-Space/Two-Space Option

GDP offers the option of typing one space or two spaces after punctuation: periods (at ends of sentences only), question marks, exclamation points, and colons. This option is set on a class-wide level by your instructor, and affects all scored activities, including document processing exercises. Check with your instructor, as typing one space after punctuation when the setting is for two spaces (and vice-versa) will result in scoring errors.

2.9 | Types of Exercises in GDP

The exercises in GDP parallel those in the textbook. The software can time, score, repeat an exercise, diagnose (and recommend corrective practice), deliver instruction, and provide directions for the exercises. The major types of exercises are described briefly in this section.

2.9.1 Warmups

Each lesson begins with a Warmup activity (with the exception of Lesson 1), consisting of drills to loosen the fingers. Warmups reinforce learned alphabet, number and symbol keys.

Warmup activities are recorded but not scored. They are listed as completed in the Student Portfolio, and your typed text is available in the Detailed Report.

The Warmup screen consists of a large typing area. Type the Warmup from copy displayed in your textbook. Begin typing when you are ready. Type the Warmup text two times. Click **Next** to continue.

If the Warmup is not typed twice, a GDP message will advise you that the exercise is not completed. Check with your instructor to determine whether you should complete the exercise or proceed to the next activity. Click **Continue with this exercise** to complete the Warmup. Click **Proceed to the next exercise** if you choose to move on to the lesson exercise that follows the Warmup.

2.9.2 New Key Drills

New Key drills introduce you to new keyboard characters. As you sequence through the instruction screens, GDP tells you which finger to use for each new key and provides a multimedia demonstration of the correct keyboarding for the character. As you progress through the exercise, you will type several lock-stepped sequences of the new keys, which require you to type the correct key before continuing. Once the lock-stepped lines are completed, you advance to scored New Key drill lines. Both the lock-stepped and the scored text results can be reviewed in your Student Portfolio.

The New Key drill screen displays the text that is to be typed above the input area. Textual instructions appear on the left side of the screen, and a keyboard map appears below the input area. Word Wrap is off for the New Key drills.

2.9.3 Other Drills

Drills other than new key exercises generally focus on either speed or accuracy.

Accuracy Pattern

Each group of practice lines is typed twice:

```
jamb   lamb   limb   limp   lump   bump   pump   jump
pals   pale   sale   same   sane   vane   cane   cape
cure   core   cove   wove   move   more   mare   maze


jamb   lamb   limb   limp   lump   bump   pump   jump
pals   pale   sale   same   sane   vane   cane   cape
cure   core   cove   wove   move   more   mare   maze
```

Speed Pattern

Each practice line is typed twice before proceeding to the next line:

```
jamb   lamb   limb   limp   lump   bump   pump   jump
jamb   lamb   limb   limp   lump   bump   pump   jump

pals   pale   sale   same   sane   vane   cane   cape
pals   pale   sale   same   sane   vane   cane   cape

cure   core   cove   wove   move   more   mare   maze
cure   core   cove   wove   move   more   mare   maze
```

2.9.4 Timed Writings

There are several types of timed writings in GDP, including 12-second speed sprints and 1- to 5-minute timed writings in lesson exercises (accessible from the Lessons menu) plus additional Open, Custom, and Supplementary timed writings (accessible from the Timed Writings and Skillbuilding menus only). All types of timed writings work essentially the same:

1. Select the timed writing from the lesson exercise folder on the Lessons menu or from one of the timed writings folders on the Timed Writings or Skillbuilding menu. In some cases, you are allowed to choose the timed writing duration.

2. After reading the introductory/instruction screens, turn to the appropriate passage in the textbook and begin typing when you are ready. (For Custom Timed Writings, you must have printed text because Custom Timed Writings are not included in the textbook. Any text can be used for Open Timed Writings; Open Timed Writings are scored for speed only.)

3. Type the copy and, if finished typing the passage before time is up, press **Enter** and begin typing the passage again. Depending on your Full Editing in Timed Writings setting (see 2.2 Specifying Your Settings on page 11), the mouse and standard editing keys may or may not be enabled for editing. Note: The screen timer begins with your first keystroke.

Note	For timed writings that allow you to restart during the first 15 seconds, a beep indicates when the restart period is over. For 3- and 5-minute timed writings, a beep signals when 30 seconds remain. For all timed writings, a beep signals when time is up.

4. When time is up, the copy is scored for both speed and accuracy (except for Open Timed Writings, which are scored for speed only). Your scores will display at the top of the screen.

5. Review the scored copy to pinpoint errors.

6. If desired, you can repeat the timed writing.

Note	For information on the formula used to calculate speed or the way errors are marked in scored copy, see 3.4 Scoring and Error Marking on page 48.

2.9.5 Pretest/Practice/Posttest

Many lessons include a Pretest, Practice, and Posttest three-step routine that identifies speed and accuracy needs and measures improvement. The Pretest/Practice/Posttest activities can be accessed from the Lessons menu and from the Skillbuilding menu.

The Pretest is a preliminary 1-minute, scored timed writing that targets a specific typing technique and is used to determine your initial skill level. Practices are unscored drills that reinforce the skill tested. The Posttest is a repeat of the Pretest. Your goal is to improve your Pretest score when you take the Posttest. Results of your Pretests and Posttests, as well as your typed text, are available in your Student Portfolio.

2.9.6 Document Processing

Documents in the Textbook

GDP links to Word 2000, 2002, 2003, or 2007 for document processing exercises. That link is specified in your Settings under the Options drop-down menu.

To produce a document in the textbook, select the document from the Lessons menu. The MS Word Document Options dialog box displays your options for the file to be used for the exercise: choose an option, and GDP links to Word.

Unless otherwise instructed, you should use Word's default settings. Type the document and proofread and spell-check it.

When finished working on the document, exit Word by selecting *Return to GDP* on the GDP menu. A dialog box asks if you want to save the file; you must click **Yes** in order for the document to be saved. If this is a scored exercise, the next dialog box asks if you want the document scored. If the document is incomplete, you should click **No**. If it is complete, clicking **Yes** will score the document and give you an opportunity to review the scored text.

Documents are scored for keystrokes only, not for formatting. Make sure to print a copy of the final document so that your instructor can score it for formatting. If you print the document within Word (before returning to GDP), exercise time on task accumulates while the document is printing, and the document prints without a header (your name, class, and date information). Another printing method, which includes a header and does not add time to the exercise, is to print the document from your Portfolio. To do so, access your Portfolio (from the File drop-down menu or the toolbar), select the document from the Student Portfolio, click **View Text**, and then click **Print in MS Word**.

MS Word Document Options Dialog Box

GDP launches the MS Word Document Options dialog when the **Next** button is clicked from a document processing instruction-screen. The document opened automatically has the correct file name when GDP launches it. Do not change the file name unless instructed to do so in your text, or scoring errors may result.

The MS Word Document Options dialog uses the following buttons to open a named document in Word. A disabled (gray) button indicates that those options are not currently available for this activity.

> **Create (document file name)** -- Click **Create** to open a blank, named document.
> Note: The Edit button will be active if you have already worked on this document. Clicking **Create** will delete your previous effort on this exercise and open a blank, named document.

> **Edit (document file name)** -- Click the **Edit** button to open and revise a file you have already typed.

> **Open (document file name) to create (document file name)** -- Some document processing activities involve editing files typed in other exercises. Clicking this button opens a copy of the specified "Open" file from another exercise and creates (renames) it as the current exercise file name. Your original file (the "Open" file) is not altered.

GDP-Word Interface

When the **Create**, **Edit**, or **Open** buttons are clicked on the MS Word Document Options dialog, GDP launches Word. GDP's Word interface adds the *GDP* drop-down menu to Word's toolbar (to the right of Help).

The GDP menu offers these choices:

> **Return to GDP** -- Click **Return to GDP** when you are ready to score your document, or when you are ready to exit Word without scoring your document and return to GDP. When this option is clicked, Word closes and you return to the lesson that you were working on when you accessed Word.

> **Reference Manual** -- The Reference Manual is a separate help system that offers examples of formatted documents, as well as format instructions. If you would like formatting help while you work on a document, click **Reference Manual**.

> **Hide Proofreading Viewer** -- This option displays only if you enabled the Proofreading Viewer in your settings from the *Options* drop-down menu. The Proofreading Viewer launches a Read-Only version of scored text, and is available only when you use the **Edit** button (in the MS Word Document Options dialog) to revise a previously scored document. Click **Hide Proofreading Viewer** if you do not want to see a Read-Only version of your scored text.

Use Word's Help system if you have questions about Word functionality. Use the Reference Manual if you want to review examples of formatted documents.

Documents Not in the Textbook

To create documents NOT in the textbook, you can link to Word by selecting *Go To Word Processor* from the File drop-down menu.

When you create documents this way, you will have to create a name for and save the document within Word. It is recommended that you use a separate data disk for documents not included in the textbook.

For more information, see 2.4.1 Linking to Word Outside of an Exercise on page 18.

2.9.7 Language Arts

These exercises are designed to help you improve language skills for business. Typically, a language arts exercise introduces a rule, illustrates its use by giving examples, then pretests your knowledge by asking you to apply the rule in a particular passage. If you make one or more errors on the pretest, GDP takes you through a tutorial that re-introduces the rule and gives illustrations, then presents a series of sentences to edit or a series of multiple-choice questions to answer. Language arts exercises can be accessed through the Lessons menu or through the Language Arts menu.

2.9.8 Diagnostic Practice

Diagnostic Practices are used to evaluate your weaknesses on keys and then provide exercises to help you maintain an expected WPM and error limit. These exercises are timed and scored and include a Pretest/Practice/Posttest sequence. GDP performs a diagnostic analysis on errors to indicate weak or error-prone fingers and prescribe additional typing drills, printed in the textbook reference section, based on the type and number of errors diagnosed.

2.9.9 Progressive Practice

Progressive Practice exercises are a series of 30-second timed writing that will help you increase both speed and accuracy. Progressive Practice: Alphabet exercises concentrate on keying all of the letters of the alphabet, while Progressive Practice: Numbers focus on keying numerical expressions and words. The timed writings range from 16 to 104 wpm (words per minute).

A 1-minute entry timed writing is taken to establish your beginning speed goal. The error limit for the 1-minute timed writing is three or fewer errors. Once the entry timed writing is scored, GDP will present a Progressive Practice paragraph that is 2 wpm faster than your most recently achieved goal (each passage increases incrementally in speed by 2 wpm). Your goal is to key the passage within 30 seconds with no errors. When you have achieved that goal, GDP will promote you to the next passage so that you can increase your speed and accuracy skills

Once your speed for the Progressive Practice has been established, a GDP message dialog displays when Progressive Practice is chosen from a menu. The message reminds you that you will begin at the speed of your last achieved goal. Progressive Practices can be accessed from either a lesson menu or from the Skillbuilding menu.

2.9.10 Paced Practice

One of the best ways to develop speed and control errors is through the use of paced exercises. The Paced Practice paragraphs in GDP are written to contain an exact number of words to be typed within two minutes. Your goal is to complete each paragraph within two minutes with no more than two errors. When you achieve your speed and accuracy goals, GDP progresses you to the next, more difficult, paragraph. Because each paragraph is longer than the previous one, you are forced to push yourself to the next higher speed. To help pace yourself, the paragraph contains quarter-minute markers.

Paced Practices build speed and accuracy by using individualized goals and immediate feedback. This exercise (accessed from the Skillbuilding menu) consists of a series of two-minute timed writings for speeds ranging from 16 to 96 wpm (words per minute). You will type timed passages with red goal markers at 15-second intervals. A 1-minute entry timed writing that establishes your base speed is taken the first time Paced Practice is attempted. Paced Practice routines incorporate both speed and accuracy goals. Your results can be seen in both the Student Portfolio and the Detailed Report.

2.9.11 Sustained Practice

Sustained Practices consist of four paragraphs. Begin the activity by opening your textbook to the Sustained Practice and typing the *first* Sustained Practice paragraph; you take a 1-minute timed writing on the first paragraph. You are expected to complete the paragraph with three or fewer errors to establish your base speed. If you have more than three errors, you repeat the paragraph until it is completed within the error goal. Once your base speed has been established, you take up to four one-minute timed writings on the remaining three paragraphs. As soon as you equal or exceed the base speed within the error limit (three errors) on one paragraph, the software advances you to the next, slightly more difficult paragraph. To complete the first attempt, type the *second* Sustained Practice paragraph in your textbook. To advance to the third paragraph in your textbook, you must type the second paragraph in one minute with three or fewer errors. Sustained Practice exercises are accessible from both the Lessons and Skillbuilding menus.

2.9.12 Technique Practice

There are two basic types of Technique Practices: Keys and Concentration. Technique Practices for keys (including the Backspace, Colon, Enter, Hyphen, Question Mark, Shift, Shift/Caps Lock, Space Bar, and Tab keys) are designed to help you consciously practice the efficient, touch-typed reach for each key. Concentration Technique Practice is designed to help you keep your eyes on the copy, not on the keyboard. These practices are unscored, untimed, and similar to warmups. Technique Practices are accessed from either the Lessons menu or from the Skillbuilding menu. Text typed for Technique Practices can be reviewed in the Student Portfolio.

2.9.13 Proofreading and Spelling

Proofreading activities allow you to practice your proofreading skills by making corrections to incorrectly keyed passages. You are instructed to edit the passage on screen to correct any keyboarding or formatting errors. The Spelling activity provides you with the opportunity to practice typing words correctly, as well as to edit incorrectly spelled words. Both types of activities are scored.

Documents designated as Proofreading Checks in the textbook serve as a check of your proofreading skill. Your goal is to have zero typographical errors when GDP first scores the document. You can find this information in the document heading under Attempt.

2.9.14 Numeric Keypad

The numeric keypad exercises, which are accessible from the Skillbuilding menu only, teach you how to use the numeric keypad and build skills in typing numbers. There are three sections of numeric keypad exercises:

- **Introduction** exercises teach the keys on the numeric keypad. They are very similar to new key drills on the standard keyboard.
- **Pretest/practice/posttest** sequences resemble other pretest/practice/posttest sequences, except that you type numbers in right-justified columns rather than text in a blank input screen.
- **Practice** exercises are additional, scored exercises that focus on particular kinds of numbers (e.g., long decimal numbers).

The timing and scoring of numeric keypad exercises differs from those of text-based exercises. Time in numeric keypad exercises is recorded as the number of seconds it takes you to complete the exercise (e.g., S 193 means that you took 193 seconds to complete the exercise). Speed in numeric keypad exercises is reported in digits per minute (e.g., 101 DPM).

Note	On screen, numbers with four or more digits appear with commas to make reading easier. You should not type the comma or scoring errors will occur.

2.9.15 MAP (Misstroke Analysis and Prescription)

MAP is a special activity that identifies keystroking problems and prescribes remedial exercises to help you fix those problems. This activity is not found in the textbook and is accessible from the MAP and Skillbuilding menus.

To work on the MAP activity, you first take a pretest and have the pretest scored. The MAP program analyzes your pretest, shows a detailed breakdown of pretest results, and recommends up to four different prescriptive drills that should help you avoid making similar errors in the future. (If you made more than four different types of errors, MAP shows the top four problems that need addressing.) You can then work on the prescriptive drills.

2.9.16 Tennis Game

The tennis game is an interactive game designed to help you improve speed, accuracy, and concentration on the keyboard. The tennis game is accessible from the Games and Skillbuilding menus. Results from completed matches are saved by GDP and appear in your Portfolio.

Before playing the tennis game, you set up the game using the Tennis Game Options screen. On this screen, you specify a Skill Level (from 1 to 5 – the skill level determines the speed of play, with 5 being the fastest speed), Number of Sets (1 or 3, with each set consisting of six games), Sound (on or off), Demonstration Mode (you select this option to see the Tennis Game operate by itself), and Select the Game Keys (Select Learned Keys, All Keys, by Fingers, by Hand, by Row, or individually selected – selected keys are highlighted in green).

Playing the Tennis Game

To begin playing the game, click the **Next** arrow on the Tennis Options screen. The Tennis Game screen opens. Two players appear on the play screen: your player is in the left court and your opponent is in the right court. The scoreboard appears at the top of the screen. To begin the game and serve the ball, press **Enter**. The ball is served to your opponent's court. When your opponent returns the serve, a keyboard character appears on screen in a white box covering part of the net. The goal is for you to type that character as quickly as possible.

- If you type the correct character before the ball crosses the net, your player wins the point.
- If you type the correct character after the ball crosses the net but before the ball reaches your player, no point is scored and the rally continues.
- If you type the wrong character or type the correct character but after the ball reaches your player, the opponent wins the point.

After each point, you press **Enter** to serve for the next point. At the end of a game, the scoreboard is updated and the next game begins. At the end of the match (i.e., after either 1 or 3 sets), the winner is announced, your scores are recorded in the Student Portfolio, and the program asks if you want a rematch.

Scoring follows standard tennis rules. A game is won by the first person to win 4 points (15, 30, 40, game), but must be won by at least two points. The score for a game tied at 40 to 40 is called "deuce," and the score for a player who has one point more than the other player (above 40) is called "advantage." A set is won by the first player to win 6 games, but must be won by at least two games. At any time during the match, you can review the rules of the game by clicking the **Rules** button in the bottom right-hand corner of the play screen.

At any time during the game, you can exit by pressing **Esc** or clicking an active toolbar button. If the match is incomplete, GDP does not save the results.

2.9.17 Pace Car Game

One of the best ways to develop speed and control errors is through the use of paced exercises. The Pace Car game uses the same paragraphs as Paced Practice. The Pace Car activity is an interactive game that uses a race car game to help you build speed and accuracy. This game is accessible from the Games menu and from the Skillbuilding menu. Results from completed games are saved by GDP and appear in your Portfolio.

The game can be played in either Paced or Sprint mode. In Paced mode, the paragraphs are written to contain an exact number of words to be typed within two minutes. Your goal is to complete each paragraph within two minutes with no more than one error (The screen shows a pace car just ahead of your car, and the object is to keep up with, but not overtake, the pace car.). In Sprint mode, the screen shows cars that are faster and slower than your car, and the object is to type as quickly and as accurately as possible in order to pass the cars ahead of you. When you achieve your speed and accuracy goals, GDP progresses you to the next, more difficult, paragraph. Because each paragraph is longer than the previous one, you are forced to push yourself to the next higher speed.

Playing the Pace Car Game

Before playing the game for the first time, you will take a 1-minute entry timed writing to determine your beginning speed. Type the paragraph. If you finish before time is up, press **Enter** and start typing the paragraph a second time. When time is up, the game begins. (If your entry timed writing has too many errors, GDP will have you retake the entry timed writing so that a more appropriate beginning speed can be used for the game.) When playing the game in Paced mode, you try to keep up with, but not overtake, the pace car. If you type too quickly, you will collide with the pace car and be penalized. When playing the game in Sprint mode, you type the text as quickly and as accurately as possible in order to pass cars ahead of your car. If you finish before time is up in either version of the pace car game, press **Enter** and start retyping the paragraph.

When time is up, your text is scored and you are given the opportunity to review your scored text. At any time during the game, you can exit by pressing **Esc** or clicking an active toolbar button. If you do not finish the game, GDP does not save your results.

2.9.18 Tests

The timed writing tests and the document processing tests for each part of the textbook are accessible from the Lessons menu after the last lesson in a part (group of 20 lessons). The part tests are included in your textbook. If you are taking an alternate part test, be sure to get the text from your instructor. The easiest way to access a test is to click the *Tests Only* link on the Lessons menu. Click the down arrow next to the test name field to open the Test drop-down menu. Click on a test to open its menu.

Tests are available for Parts 2 through 6. When you are ready to take a test, notify your instructor to be sure you have the correct material needed for the test.

The results of the timed writing tests will be recorded in your Portfolio and the copy will be treated like any other completed exercise. Document processing tests are scored for keystrokes only. Be sure to print a copy of these documents so that your instructor can check formatting manually.

3.1 | GDP Drop-Down Menus

Drop-down menus can be accessed from the menu bar running across the top of the GDP screen.

3.1.1 File Menu

Portfolio...	Use *Portfolio...* to view or print a report showing your scores on completed GDP exercises as well as scored text for any exercise. The report can be restricted by date range, lesson number, or exercise type.
Performance Chart...	Use *Performance Chart...* to view or print a graph showing your speed and accuracy on all timed writings in a part (group of 20 lessons).*
Import Student Data...	This feature is used to import data from one GDP location to another to allow for working on GDP in multiple locations.*
Export Student Data...	This feature is used to create an export file of your data, which can then be imported into GDP on another workstation (for example, if you work on GDP in more than one location.)*
Go To Word Processor	Use *Go To Word Processor* to link to Microsoft Word 2000, 2002, 2003, or 2007 to work on documents that are not included in the textbook or print copies of completed documents without accessing those documents through the Lessons menu.
E-mail Instructor...	Use *E-mail Instructor...* to create and send an e-mail message to your instructor.
Delete Files	Use *Delete Files* to delete your text for selected lessons and exercise types.*
Exit GDP	Use *Exit GDP* to exit the program.*

*If this feature is inactive on your menu, press **Escape** or click the Lessons icon to return to the Lessons menu.

Note	When *Delete Files* is used, just your scored text is deleted. Scores are maintained in your Portfolio, but the asterisk preceding the date in the Student Profile (indicating that a Detailed Report is available) is removed.

3.1.2 Options Menu

Personal Information...	Use *Personal Information...* to enter information such as your initials, a byline, and e-mail address for distance-learning features. GDP opens the Personal Information form when you need to add or change information.
Settings...	Use *Settings...* to specify browser, word processing, and certain other settings for using GDP.

3.1.3 Help Menu

Program Overview	Use *Program Overview* for a quick text-only introduction to GDP.
Reference Manual	Use *Reference Manual* for detailed instructions on formatting the various types of documents produced in GDP.
Tutorial	Use *Tutorial* to take a short multimedia tour of the GDP program and learn how it works.
MAP Slide Show	Use *MAP Slide Show* to directly access the multi media tutorial that explains GDP's Misstroke Analysis and Prescription program (This tutorial is also accessible via the **View MAP Slide Show** button on the MAP introduction screen.).
Help	Use *Help* to view the contents tab for Help topics.
Live Update	Use *Live Update* to see if any new updates are available for GDP (Note: You will be notified automatically if this is checked off within your settings.).
About...	Use *About...* to determine which version of the program is being used. This information is useful when calling customer support.

3.2 | GDP Toolbar

The toolbar is a row of buttons running across the top of the GDP screen across the navigation menu. Use the toolbar for quick access to frequently used features and on-screen guidance. When you rest the mouse pointer over a button on the toolbar, a Tooltip shows the name of the button and the keyboard shortcut, if there is one. See 3.3 Keyboard Shortcuts.

Upload

Use this button, which is active in all GDP 10th Edition versions, to send your data files to the Instructor Management Web site.

E-mail

Use this button to create and send an e-mail message to your instructor.

Web

Use this button to access your campus Web site, if a URL is specified in your settings.

Portfolio

Use this button to access your reports.

Reference Manual

Use this button for help with formatting the various types of documents included in GDP.

Help

Use this button to get information about how GDP works.

3.3 | Keyboard Shortcuts

Sometimes it is easier to use a keyboard shortcut rather than to remove your hand from the keyboard to activate the mouse. Here are the keyboard shortcuts in GDP:

Alt	**Menu bar** Activates the menu bar.
Alt+→	**Next** Moves to the next screen in an exercise.
Alt+←	**Previous** Moves back to the previous screen in an exercise.
Ctrl+A	**Language Arts menu** Opens the Language Arts menu.
Ctrl+G	**Games menu** Opens the Games menu.
Ctrl+L	**Lessons menu** Opens the Lessons menu.

Ctrl+M	**MAP program** Opens the MAP program.
Ctrl+P	**Portfolio** Provides access to student reports.
Ctrl+R	**Restart timed writing** Allows the student to restart most timed writings within the first 15 seconds.
Ctrl+S	**Skillbuilding menu** Opens the Skillbuilding menu.
Ctrl+Shft+M	**Reference Manual** Provides formatting guidelines for various types of documents.
Ctrl+T	**Timed Writings menu** Opens the Timed Writings menu.
Ctrl+X	**Exit** Exits the program. Not active within an exercise (press **Esc** to cancel the exercise first).
Esc	**Previous Menu** Cancels an exercise. If a scored exercise, the report is marked canceled.
F1	**Help** Opens Help.

3.4 | Scoring and Error Marking

3.4.1 Error Marking

Errors in scored copy are marked as follows:

- **Underlined red**: all incorrect words.
- **<green in angle brackets>**: all omitted words, tabs (designated as **<[T]>**), and hard returns (designated as **<¶>**).
- **{Blue in braces}**: incorrectly inserted words, tabs (designated as **{[T]}**), and hard returns (designated as **{¶}**).

Examples	Incorrect word	You **cane** go.
	Omitted word	You <**can** >go
	Inserted word	You {**perhaps**}can go
	Inserted Tab	{**[T]**}You can go.
	Omitted tab	<**[T]**>You can go.
	Inserted hard return	You can go.{**¶**}
	Omitted hard return	You can go.<**¶**>

3.4.2 One-Space/Two-Space Option

GDP offers the option of typing one space or two spaces after punctuation: periods (at ends of sentences only), question marks, exclamation points, and colons. This option is set on a class-wide level by your instructor, and affects all scored activities, including document processing exercises. Check with your instructor, as typing one space after punctuation when the setting is for two spaces (and vice-versa) will result in scoring errors. The default in your settings allows for one space between sentences.

3.4.3 Error Scores

The most widely used rules for determining the error score on a timed writing are the International Typewriting Contest Rules. According to these rules, every actual word that differs from the original source copy counts as 1 error. The determination of errors by GDP is based on these rules.

3.4.4 Speed (WPM) Calculation

In all but numeric keypad exercises, GDP calculates, displays, and records your speed as wpm—that is, as words per minute. A word equals 5 keystrokes (letters, spaces, tabs, hard returns, etc.). Like all other scores, each wpm score is based on the copy in the book: incorrectly added strokes are not counted; similarly, incorrectly omitted strokes are not subtracted.

The words-per-minute (wpm) speed is based on the following formulas.

- 12-second timed writings: Each letter or space counts as 1 wpm.
- 30-second timed writings: Every 5 keystrokes (letters, spaces, tabs, and hard returns) count as 2 wpm.
- Minute timed writings: The total number of 5-letter words is divided by the number of minutes in the timed writing.

$$25 \text{ words} \div 1 \text{ minute} = 25 \text{ wpm}$$
$$50 \text{ words} \div 2 \text{ minutes} = 25 \text{ wpm}$$
$$75 \text{ words} \div 3 \text{ minutes} = 25 \text{ wpm}$$
$$125 \text{ words} \div 5 \text{ minutes} = 25 \text{ wpm}$$

Note	Speed in numeric keypad exercises is reported in seconds, corresponding to the number of seconds it takes you to complete the exercise. For example, S 193 indicates that it took you 193 seconds to complete the exercise.

Chapter 4   *Troubleshooting*

If you have any questions or problems as you install GDP or work with your data files, first make sure that your system meets the requirements outlined in 1.2 System Requirements on page 1 and that you followed the exact procedure outlined in 1.4 Installing GDP on page 3. Next, check this troubleshooting guide. If you experience a problem not covered here or not remedied by following a suggestion listed here, record exactly at what point in the program the problem occurred and a description of what happened when you encountered the problem. Then call McGraw-Hill's technical support group at **1-800-331-5094** (8 A.M.–5 P.M. CST).

4.1 | Installation and Start-Up

Problem: When installing GDP, the Select Destination Location dialog box indicates that the drive does not have sufficient free space.

> *Explanation:*   GDP requires approximately 175 MB of free hard-disk space, which the selected drive does not have.

> *Suggestion:*   If you have another hard disk drive with at least 175 MB of free space, select that other drive and click **OK** to continue the GDP installation. Otherwise, press **Esc** to cancel the installation, then free up at least 175 MB of space and run the GDP installation again.

Problem: When starting the program, a dialog box prompts you to insert a blank data disk.

> *Explanation 1:*   GDP has been configured to store student work on a floppy disk, and the program was started without a floppy disk in the floppy drive.

> *Suggestion:*   Insert a floppy disk (a blank disk if you have not yet worked with GDP or your data disk if you have already done some work in GDP) in the floppy drive.

If you do not want to store your data on floppy disks, re-install GDP and specify a different student data location.

Explanation 2:   The floppy disk is unreadable.

Suggestion: Put a new, formatted floppy disk in the floppy drive.

Problem: When starting the program, a dialog box displays an "E003 Path not found" error message.

Explanation: GDP cannot find the data directory you specified for the student data location when you installed GDP.

Suggestion: Make sure that the shortcut for the GDP program includes the full and correct path to your data files. Use Windows Explorer to verify that your data files and directories have not been moved or deleted.

Problem: Launching the program from the GDP program directory results in an error.

Explanation: The GDP program needs to know the student data location when it launches. This information is built into the program icon (shortcut) in the Keyboarding program group.

Suggestion: Always start GDP from the Start menu, selecting *Programs, Keyboarding,* and then the GDP program icon for the configuration you have installed (i.e., *GDP Home).*

4.2 | Document Processing and Scoring

Problem: For document processing exercises, GDP fails to start the word processor.

Explanation: The Microsoft Word 2000, 2002, 2003, or 2007 location specified on your settings is incorrect or is the location for a different version of the word processor.

Suggestion:	Select *Settings...* from the Options drop-down menu to access your settings. Then verify the full path to your installation of Microsoft Word 2000, 2002, 2003, or 2007.

Problem: The GDP/Return to GDP menu option in Microsoft Word 2000, 2002, 2003, or 2007 does not work.

Explanation:	Templates that are added to the startup group for Word when a Hewlett Packard printer is installed can be the cause of this problem. Hewlett Packard adds a file so that the printer can interface with HP's By Design program.
Suggestion:	Locate the file called bs2000.dot, bs2002.dot, bs2003.dot, or bs2007.dot and move it from its default location to the Templates directory.

Problem: A document or exercise does not get scored.

Explanation:	The exercise is not supposed to be scored. Practice documents, warmups, new key presentations, as well as certain practices and skillbuilding and document processing exercises are not scored.
Suggestion:	If you want to score documents manually, print copies of your documents from within Word. If you want to score other unscored exercises manually, print copies of the completed exercises from your Portfolio as follows: click the **Portfolio** button on the toolbar, specify Portfolio options, click **OK** to view the Student Portfolio, select the exercise(s) you want printed, and click **Print Text**.

Problem: Scored copy contains numerous "<¶>" or "{¶}" marks.

Explanation:	You did not follow the word wrap setting indicated in the exercise header at the top of the screen. A "<¶>" occurs in scored copy where word wrap is off and you fail to press **Enter** at the end of the line. A "{¶}" occurs in scored copy where word wrap is on and you mistakenly press **Enter** at the end of the line.
Suggestion:	Retype the exercise following the word wrap setting in the exercise header.

4.3 | Sound

Problem: No sound plays at the end of timed writings or when the restart period is over in a timed writing.

Explanation: GDP uses the Default Sound to signal the end of a timed writing and the end of the restart period. Your computer either has <none> (no audible sound) assigned to the Default Sound, or it has speakers attached to the computer but not turned on.

Suggestion: First, check to make sure that the Default Sound in your Windows Sounds control panel is assigned an audible sound such as ding, chimes, or chord. (If you are not familiar with the Sounds control panel, refer to the User's Guide for your operating system.) Also make sure that your speakers (if any are attached to your computer) are turned on and work.

4.4 | E-mail/Web

Problem: The **E-mail** button does not work on the GDP toolbar.

Explanation 1: Your system may not be configured with MAPI. When sending e-mail, GDP uses MAPI and the system's default e-mail address.

Suggestion: Make sure your computer uses a MAPI-compliant e-mail system (such as Microsoft Outlook) and that a default e-mail address is set up. Otherwise, use e-mail outside of GDP for sending and receiving e-mail messages.

Explanation 2: Either your e-mail address or the instructor's e-mail address is missing or incorrect in your settings.

Suggestion: Access GDP, then access *Settings...* from the Options drop-down menu, and enter the correct information for both your and your instructor's e-mail addresses.

Problem:	The **Web** button does not work on the GDP toolbar.

	Explanation:	The correct URL for your campus Web site is not specified in your settings.
	Suggestion:	Access GDP, then access *Settings...* from the Options drop-down menu, and enter the correct URL for your campus Web site.

4.5 Help and Reference Manual

Problem:	Clicking on the **Help** button or the **Reference Manual** button launches America Online (AOL).

	Explanation:	Both the GDP Help file and the GDP Reference Manual are composed as HTML Help files. When you launch an HTML Help file, it opens in the system's default browser. If AOL is your default Internet Service Provider (ISP), it also serves as your default browser. Therefore, opening the HTML Help file or Reference Manual will also start up AOL.
	Suggestion:	The first time you click on **Help** or **Reference Manual**, AOL will launch, in addition to the Help or Reference Manual file. Please note that you do not need to log on to AOL in order to use the Help or Reference Manual system. Minimize AOL to your taskbar instead of exiting from the program. The next time you click on **Help** or **Reference Manual**, the file will display without also displaying AOL.

4.6 Distance-Learning/Instructor Management Web Site

Problem:	When using the distance-learning feature, you are not able to upload your data to the Instructor Management Web site.

	Explanation 1:	Your Internet connection is down or the transmission is interrupted.

Suggestion:	Verify that your Internet connection is working properly outside of GDP. For example, open a browser window outside of GDP, such as Internet Explorer.
Explanation 2:	Your instructor has not yet registered you on the Instructor Management Web site.
Suggestion:	Ask your instructor to register you on the Instructor Management Web site.
Explanation 3:	Your e-mail address does not match what your instructor entered as your e-mail address on the Instructor Management Web site.
Suggestion:	Access GDP and select *Settings...* from the Options drop-down menu. Verify that your e-mail address in the Settings dialog box is correct, and tell your instructor what the correct address is. Make necessary changes in the Settings dialog box. If your e-mail address is wrong on the Instructor Management Web site, your instructor can correct it there.

4.7 Data Storage Limits

Problem: A message indicates that the data disk is full.

Explanation:	You are about to exceed the available disk space and need to free disk space before continuing.
Suggestion:	When this message appears, click **OK** to close the message dialog box. Exit GDP and make a copy of the full data disk, if you wish. Then restart GDP, and select *Delete Files* from the File drop-down menu. In the Delete Files dialog box, select the lesson(s) and exercise type(s) to delete and click **OK**. In the Confirm dialog box, click **Yes** or **Yes to All** to delete the selected files. When you delete files, you delete text (Detailed Reports) only. Scores for exercises with deleted text are retained in the Student Portfolio.

Problem: A message indicates that the Student Portfolio file is full.

Explanation:	The maximum number of exercises that can be listed

on a Student Portfolio is 1,000. When the Student Portfolio exceeds 1,000 exercises, the program automatically overwrites exercises starting with the oldest first. When this happens, you will not be able to access old exercises that are overwritten in the Student Portfolio.

Suggestion: Make a copy of the data disk (or data directory), to have in case you want to access old exercises that will not be accessible when GDP is used in the future. Then continue using GDP.

Index

NOTES